CAN YOU BELIEVE YOUR EYES ?

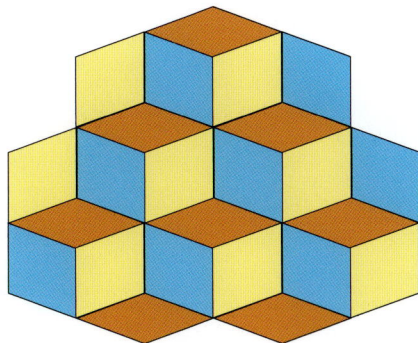

The strange world of optical illusions

Keith Gaines

OXFORD
UNIVERSITY PRESS

Great Clarendon Street, Oxford OX2 6DP

Oxford University Press is a department of the University of Oxford.
It furthers the University's objective of excellence in research, scholarship,
and education by publishing worldwide in

Oxford New York

Auckland Bangkok Buenos Aires Cape Town Chennai
Dar es Salaam Delhi Hong Kong Istanbul Karachi Kolkata
Kuala Lumpur Madrid Melbourne Mexico City Mumbai Nairobi
São Paulo Shanghai Singapore Taipei Tokyo Toronto

with an associated company in Berlin

Oxford is a registered trade mark of Oxford University Press
in the UK and in certain other countries

British Library Cataloguing in Publication Data

Data available

ISBN 0 19 917530 6

10 9 8 7 6 5 4 3 2 1

Inspection Pack (nine different titles)   ISBN 0 19 917535 7
Guided Reading Pack (six of the same title)   ISBN 0 19 917849 6
Class Pack ISBN 0 19 917536 5

Acknowledgements

The publisher would like to thank the following for permission to reproduce
photographs:

Bruce Coleman Collection/Robert Maier: p 16 (*bottom left*); Corbis Images
/Michael & Patricia Fogden: p 19 (*top right*); Corbis Images/Frank Lane Picture
Agency: p 20 (*bottom*); Corbis Images/Linda Richardshon: p 20 (*top*); Corbis
Images/Roger Tidman: p 20 (*middle*); Corbis Images/Larson Wood: p 17 (*top*);
Cordon Art/M. C. Escher 'Relativity': p 4; Cordon Art/M. C. Escher 'Sky and
Water': p 3; Corel Professional Photos: p 21 (*top*); Frank Lane Picture Agency
/Ken Day: p 18 (*middle*); Frank Lane Picture Agency/E & D Hosking: p 16 (*top*);
Frank Lane Picture Agency/Derek Middleton: p 16 (*bottom right*); Frank Lane
Picture Agency/K Aitken Panda: p 19 (*bottom*); Frank Lane Picture Agency/
A Wharton: p 18 (*bottom*); Frank Lane Picture Agency/Martin B Withers: p 17
(*middle*); Keith Gaines: pp 14 (*both*), 23, 26, 28, 29; GettyStone/Billboard: p 21
(*bottom*); GettyStone/Donna Day: p 5; Oxford Scientific Films/J. A. L. Cooke: p
19 (*top left*); Oxford Scientific Films/Carol Farneti: pp 17 (*bottom*); Geoff
Rushbrook: p 22; Martin Sookias: pp 18 (*top*), 30, 31 and back cover.

Artwork is by Peter Visscher (p 27) and Barking Dog Art.

Front cover photo: Bridgeman Art Library/Flowers Art Gallery/Patrick Hughes

Printed in Hong Kong

Contents

Introduction

Most people think that they can trust their eyes. But can they?

Look at the picture below. At first it looks like an ordinary building with stairs, doors and windows. But look more closely. Which are the floors and which are the walls? Are the stairs going up or down?

It is a trick picture. Your brain tries to make sense of what your eyes see, but the picture is confusing. No one could really build a house like this.

This picture is by an artist called M. C. Escher. The picture on page 3 is also by Escher.

Magicians rely on the fact that we usually trust our eyes. They know that our brains try to make sense of what we see, so they make sure we cannot see everything! Secret places in boxes and bags, hidden objects, quick hand movements, all help to trick our eyes, so that we believe in magic.

▲

Our eyes tell us that this man has been sawn in half. Our brains struggle to understand what has happened.

Something that tricks our eyes is called an **optical illusion**. This book is full of optical illusions. They will trick your eyes into seeing things as different sizes, shapes, and even different objects to what they really are.

Sizes

Which red line is longer?

Is it line AA at the top, or line BB at the bottom?

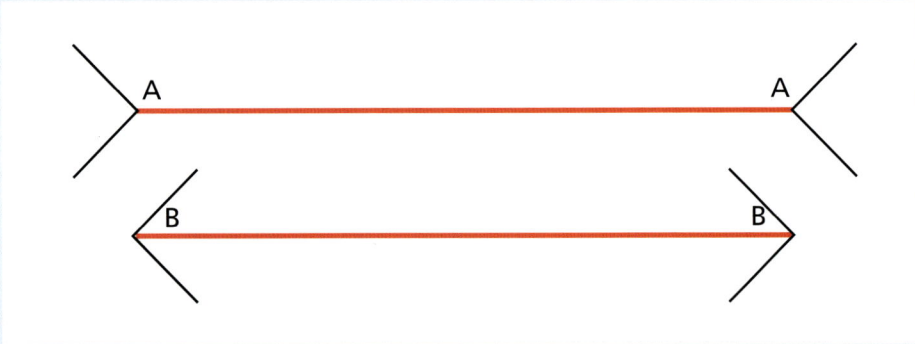

The answer is that both red lines are the same length. Measure them to check. The top red line looks longer than the bottom red line, because of the shape of the arrows on the ends. Your eyes have been tricked!

Which line is the longest?

Is it the blue line AA, the red line BB, or the green line CC?

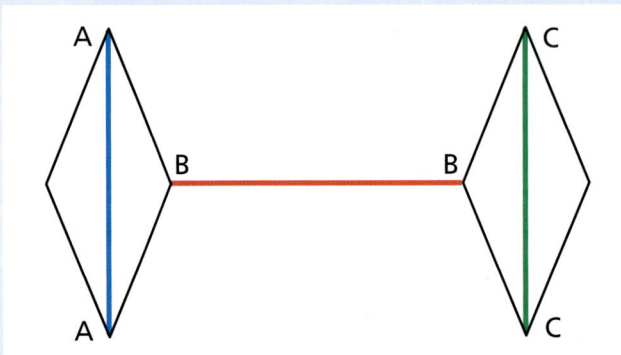

The answer is that all three lines are the same length. Measure them to check. Most people's eyes are tricked into thinking that the red line BB is the longest!

Who is the tallest?

◀ This picture shows three children running towards a door. Which one looks the tallest?

Most people will say that the one nearest the door looks the tallest.

If you take the children out of the picture and put them in a line, you will see that they are all the same height.

▼

◀ Look carefully at this picture. Which pillar looks the tallest? Use your ruler to check.

Your eyes have been tricked! As a child you learn that things which are far away normally look smaller. The lines on the ceiling, the pattern on the floor, and the windows, all tell your brain you are looking down a long corridor, so your brain thinks the pillar furthest away must be bigger than the others.

Shapes

Squashing the square

Here is a square.
All four sides are the same length.
All four sides are straight.

If you draw lots of lines
from a point outside the
square, with the lines
spreading outwards, the
right side of the same
square looks shorter
than the left side.

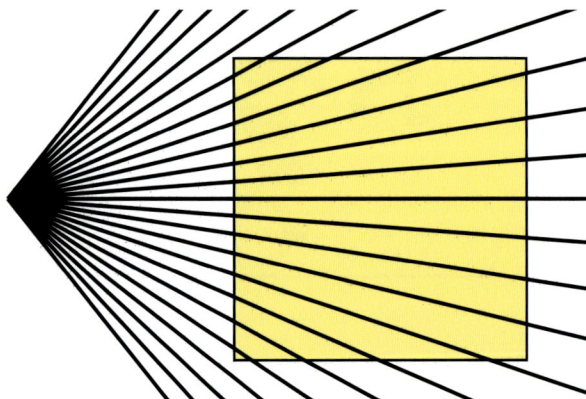

If you draw lots of circles,
with their centres in the
middle of the square, the
sides of the square seem
to bend inwards.

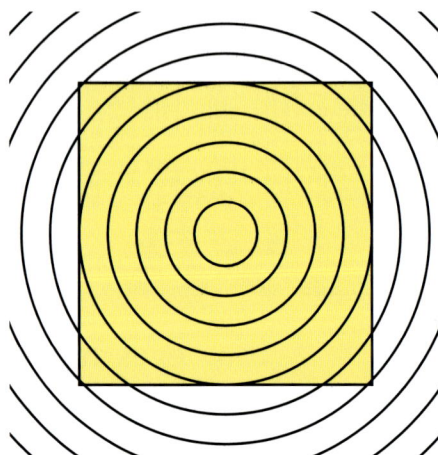

The square is exactly the same in
all three pictures. Measure it to check.

Bending the lines

Look at the two red lines AA and BB. Are they straight or bent? ▶

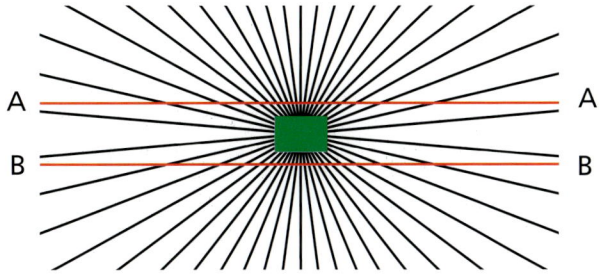

If you take away everything between the red lines, they look less bent. ▶

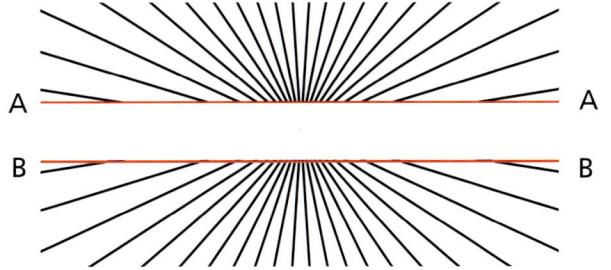

Take away all the black lines. The red lines now look straight! ▶

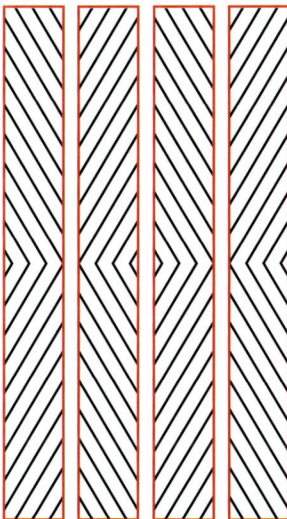

Are the sides of these red boxes straight, or are they bent? Most people will agree that they look bent.

Check the sides with a ruler. They are straight! The sloping black lines inside the boxes trick our eyes and our brains into thinking the sides of the boxes are bent.

A weird wall

Look at this wall.

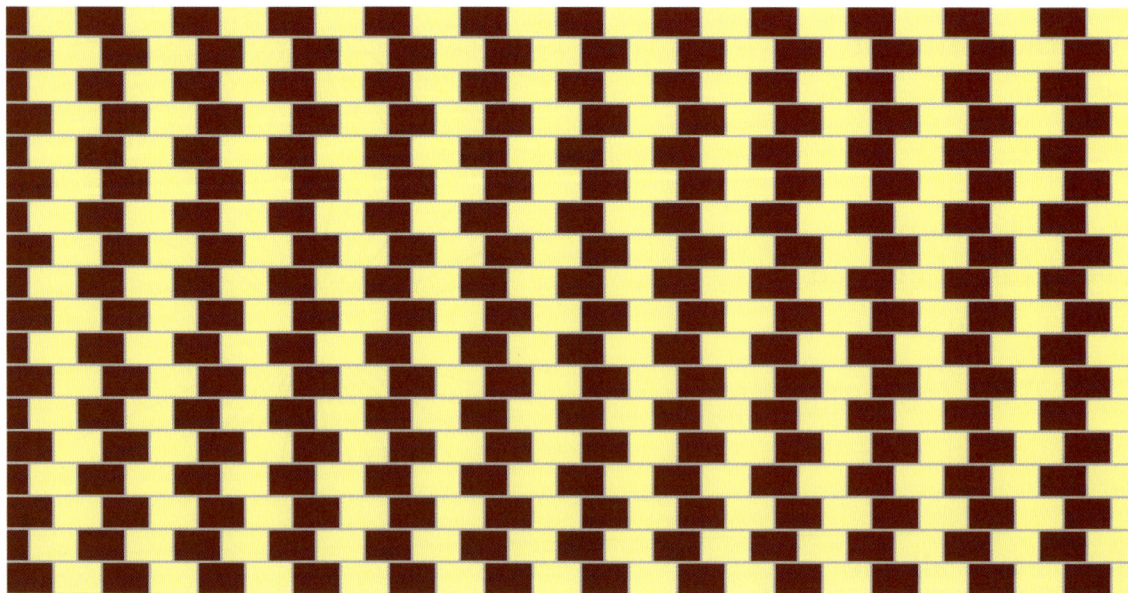

The brown and yellow bricks appear to be **wedge-shaped** rather than **rectangular**. Check them with a ruler. In fact all the bricks are rectangular!

Circles with straight sides

Hold this book about 25 cm in front of your face and look at these circles. Move the book slowly away from you. When it is about 60 cm away, each circle may seem to turn into a **hexagon**.

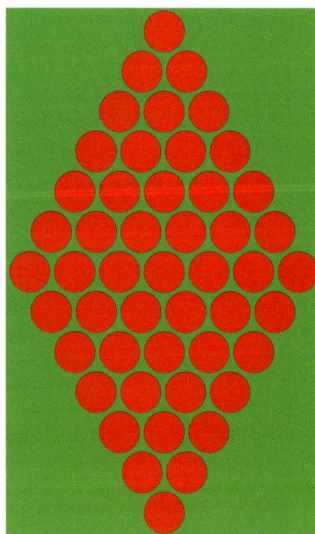

Leaning letters

The sloping lines inside ▶ these letters make them look as if they are bending over. The direction of the sloping lines changes the way we think each letter is leaning.

If we fill in the spaces ▶ between the sloping lines, the letters look straight.

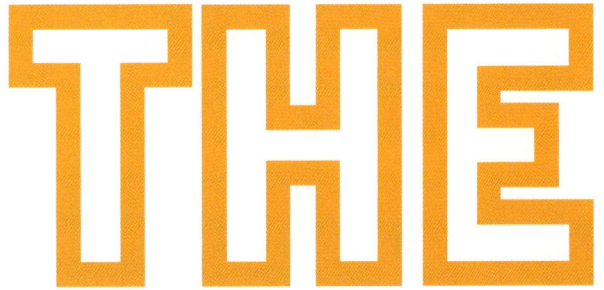

This is the title of this ▶ book, but think about the question. Your eyes tell you that the letters are crooked. They are not. It is an **optical illusion**.

THE

THE

CAN YOU
BELIEVE
YOUR
EYES?

How many?

Optical illusions can change the way we count things.

Look at this box for ten seconds.

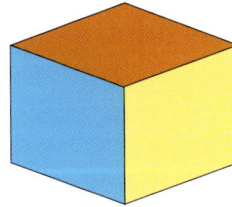

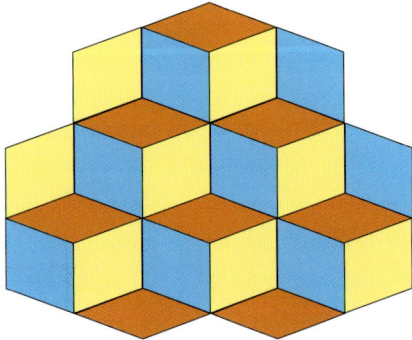

Now look at this stack of boxes. How many boxes can you see? You will probably count six boxes.

Now look at this box for ten seconds. Count the stack of boxes above. You will probably see seven boxes now!

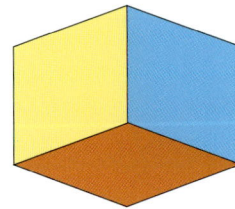

These stairs are also puzzling. Are you looking at the stairs from above or from below?

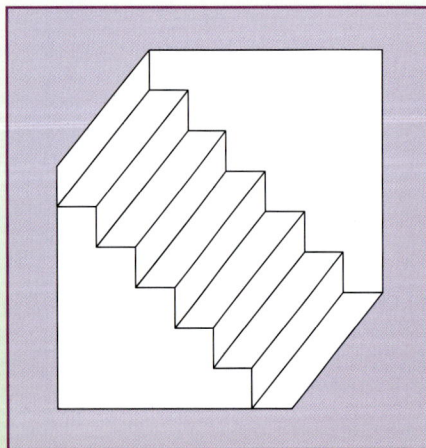

If you look down at the stairs you can see five steps.

wall

side of the stairs

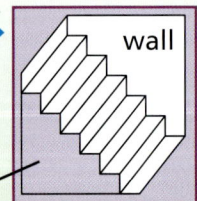

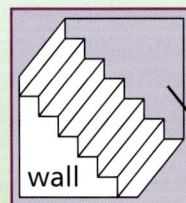

If you look up at the stairs you can see six steps!

wall

side of the stairs

The crooked arch

This is a picture of a passage with an arch at each end. There is a sign in front of it. The arch looks crooked. Is the right side of the arch lower than the left side? Will the two sides of the arch meet up at the top?

If we take away the sign, we can see that the two sides of the arch *do* match, and they meet at the top. ▼

The crooked arch (in the top picture) is an illusion. It is created because the left side of the sign post is over the exact centre of the arch. This makes the right side of the arch look much lower than it really is.

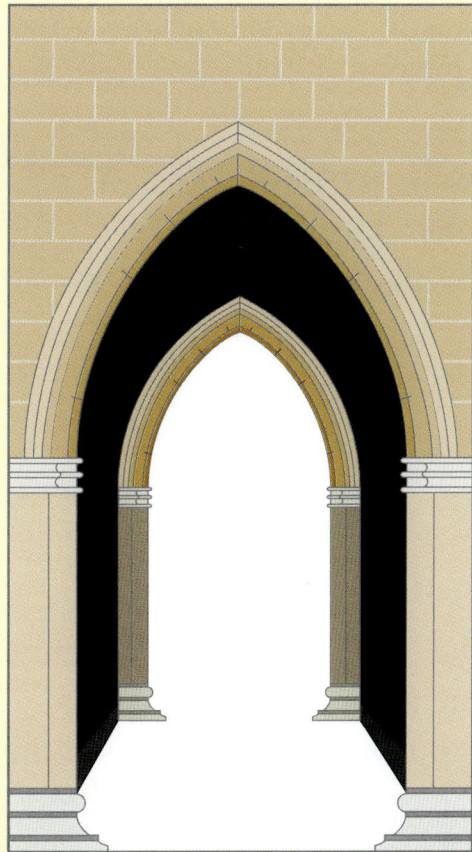

Freaky faces

◀ These Tea-pot brothers were in a children's book in the 1920s.

"I'm much bigger than you," says Tommy Tea-pot. "Yes, you are," says Timmy Tea-pot. "But my eyes are much bigger than yours."

It looks as if Timmy is right. But is he? Measure the eyes with a ruler and see if Timmy's eye really is bigger than Tommy's.

This picture was in a children's book in the 1930s. ▶

This man looks very grumpy. But you can cheer him up. Just turn the book upside-down!

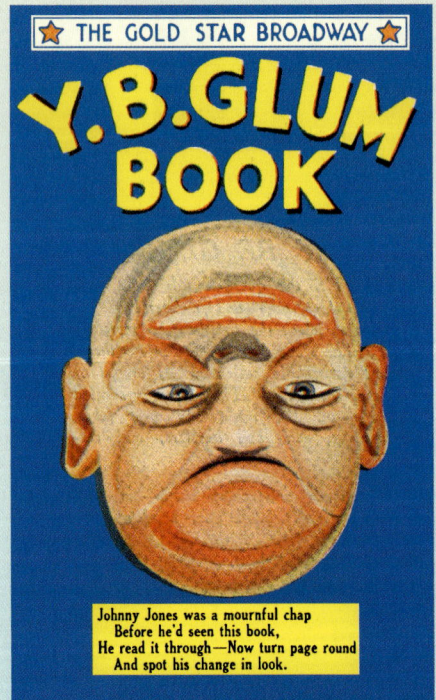

★ THE GOLD STAR BROADWAY ★

Y.B. GLUM BOOK

Johnny Jones was a mournful chap
Before he'd seen this book,
He read it through—Now turn page round
And spot his change in look.

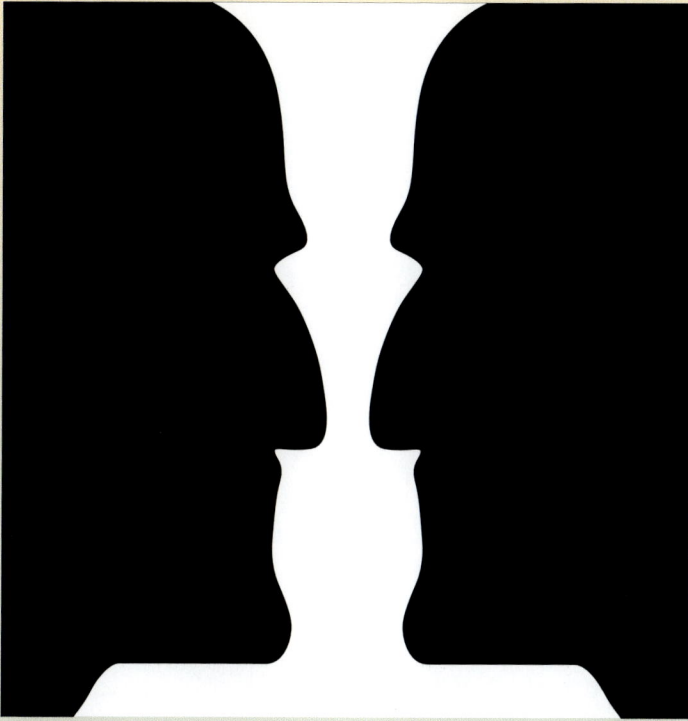

This picture shows the base of a table lamp. Or is it a candlestick? Or is it two men, face to face?

This girl is looking away from us. She is wearing earrings and a ribbon round her neck. But when she turns towards us we see an old lady – with a huge nose!

Illusions in nature

Camouflage

Many animals have skin or fur that looks like their natural background. This makes them difficult to see and is called **camouflage**.

The stripes on a tiger's coat help the tiger to blend into the long grass. ▶

Some animals change their coats to suit the season. In winter the stoat has a white coat, to blend in with the snow. In summer the stoat's coat turns brown.

▲

The stoat in winter

▲

The stoat in summer

Some frogs, fishes and reptiles can change colour depending on where they are. Their outer skin is **transparent**. Under the outer skin there are different coloured cells. These cells can change in size.

A turbot resting on the sea-bed

The turbot is a flat fish. It is usually a plain light brown colour. When it rests on the sea-bed, it takes just five minutes to change colour to blend in with the stones and sand.

A chameleon in sunlight

In sunlight, the lighter coloured cells on a chameleon's skin get bigger. This makes the chameleon look light green and brown. In shade, the lighter cells get smaller and the darker cells get bigger. This makes the chameleon's skin look darker.

A chameleon in shade

Copycat creatures

Some animals hide themselves by looking like something else.

Stick insects look like small twigs. They can stay very still, so birds cannot easily spot them.

How many stick insects can you see on this plant?

A caterpillar or a twig?

This caterpillar blends into its habitat by looking like a twig.

The leaf insect, in India, disguises itself as a leaf. It lives among leaves, so insect-eating birds cannot see it easily.

The colour and shape of the leaf insect are perfect camouflage.

American plant bugs are a family of insects that look like something else. They look like ants or thorns, so birds do not eat them.

This plant bug looks like an ant.

This plant bug looks like a thorn.

One of the strangest-looking creatures in the world is the Australian sea dragon. This sea horse curls its tail around a stalk, while it eats seaweed. It has flaps of skin which are the same colour and shape as seaweed. This hides the sea horse from big fish which would eat it.

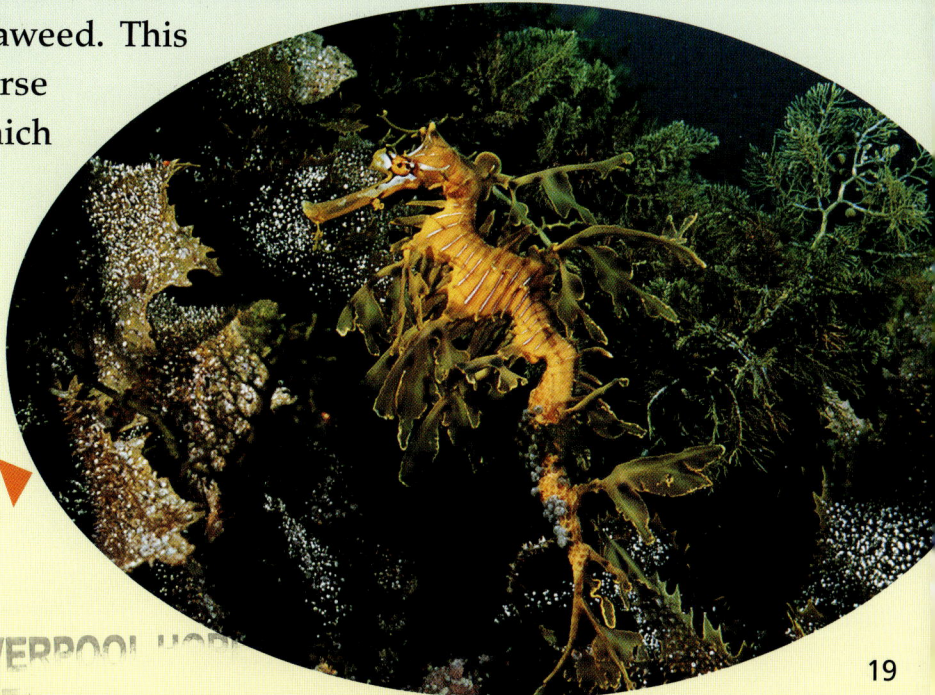

An Australian sea dragon blends into the seaweed.

Eggs and very young animals are easy prey for their enemies. They tend to be small and weak, and often they cannot move very quickly.

Some of these eggs and small animals use **optical illusions** to help them survive.

The common tern lays eggs on the seashore. The eggs look like pebbles which blend in with the shells and sand.

This tern chick is **camouflaged** among the stones on the shore.

The cuckoo lays its egg in another bird's nest. It leaves the other bird to bring up the young cuckoo. To fool the other bird, the cuckoo's egg is similar to the colour of the other bird's eggs.

lark eggs

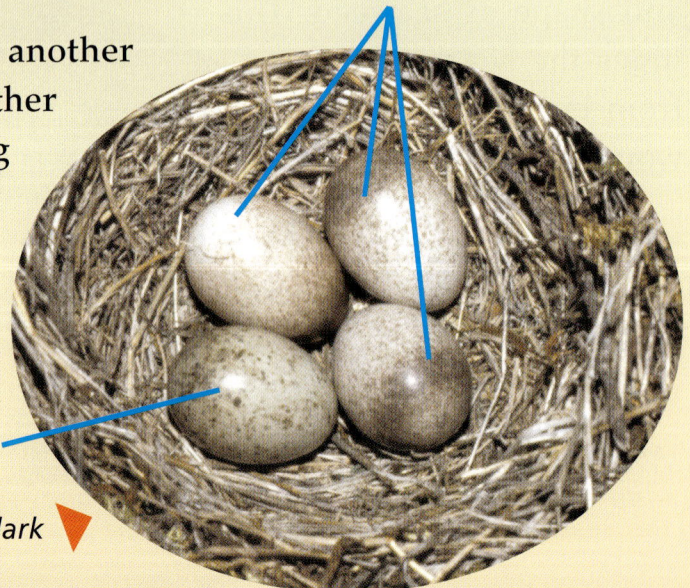

cuckoo egg

In this nest there are three lark eggs and one cuckoo egg.

Dotty pictures

Pictures in books are a type of optical illusion. They look as if they are made of solid blocks of colour or shade, but in fact they are made up of lots of different sized dots.

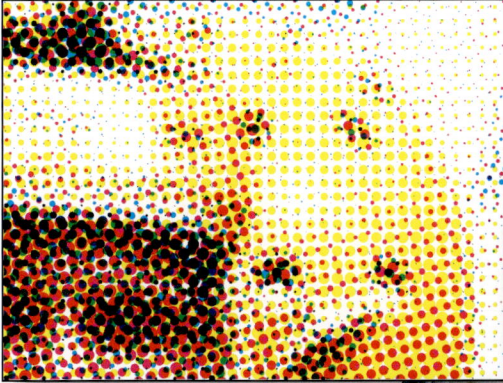

The dots in most pictures are "invisible" unless they are enlarged (see above).

Pictures on large posters are made up of large dots.

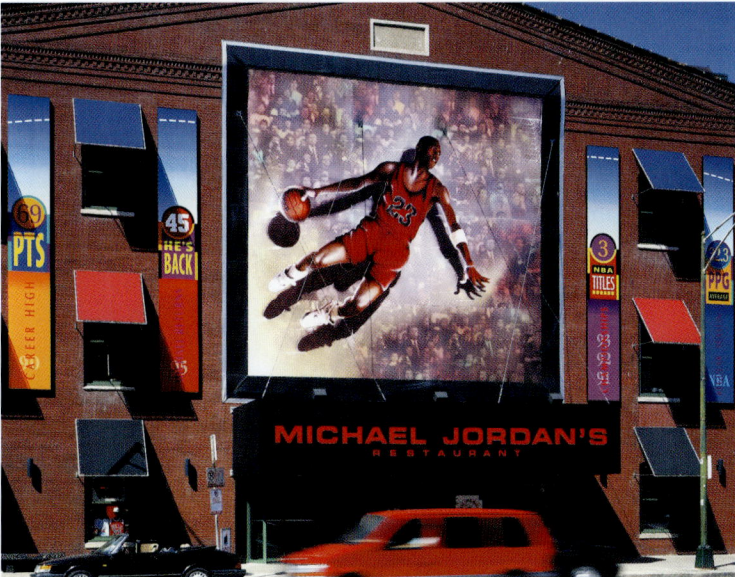

Large posters that you can see in the street are made up of much bigger dots. If you look closely at posters, you can see the separate dots.

The illusion of your TV

A television picture uses three **optical illusions**.

A normal view of a TV screen

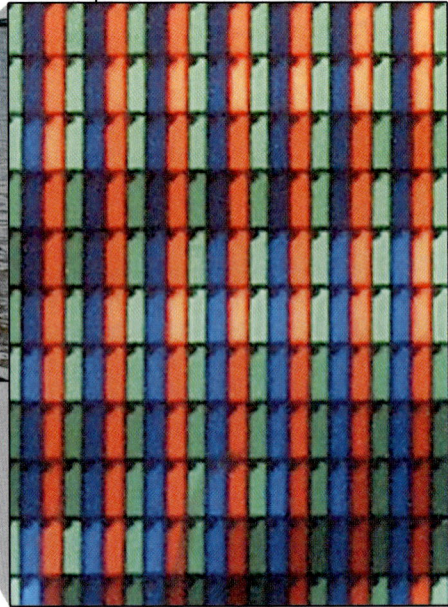

The first illusion is that the picture is made up of solid colour. It is not. It is made up of dots or small blocks of colour. Your eyes don't see the dots or blocks unless you look very closely at the screen.

A close-up view of a TV screen

The second illusion is that there are many colours on a TV screen. In fact, there are only three colours. Red, blue and green are mixed to show the whole range of colours.

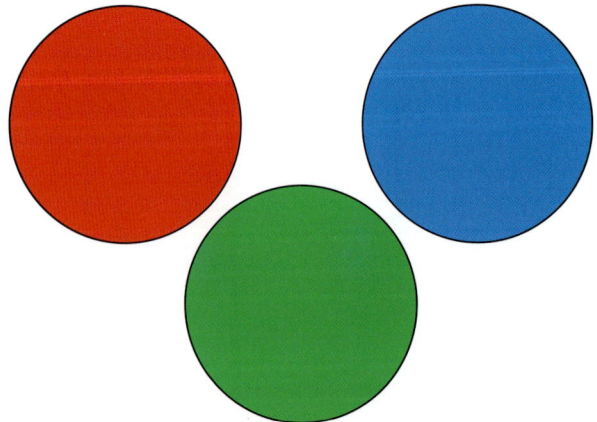

The third illusion is that the TV shows movement. However, the film is made up of 25 separate *still* pictures, shown one after another, to make each second of what looks like a moving picture.

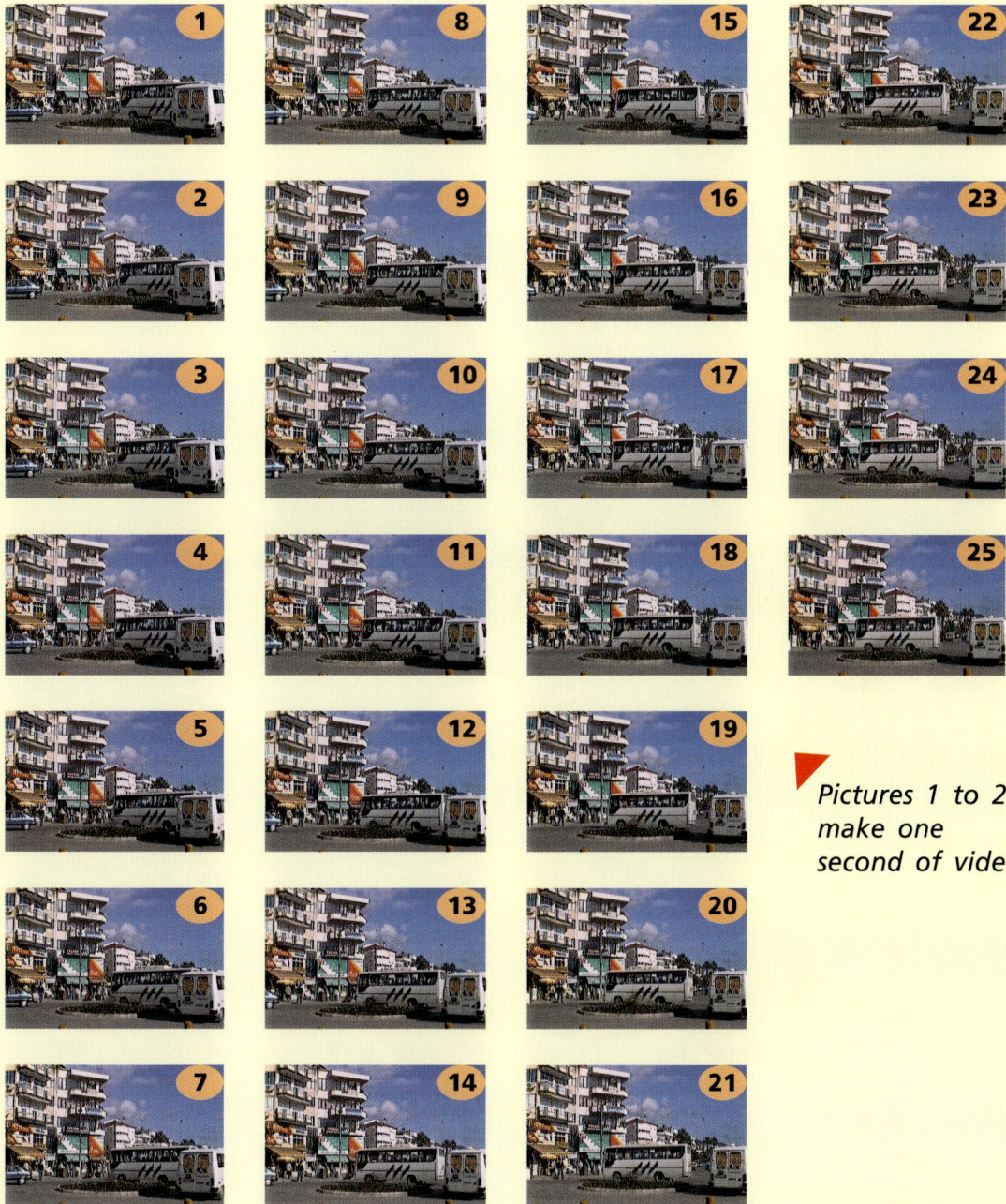

Pictures 1 to 25 make one second of video.

Confusing both eyes

Some **optical illusions** need two eyes to make them work.

1 Hold this book about 30 cm in front of your face.
2 Look at the circles below. Slowly bring the book
   closer to your face.
3 The small red circle may cross over into the big blue
   circle and fit into the white space.

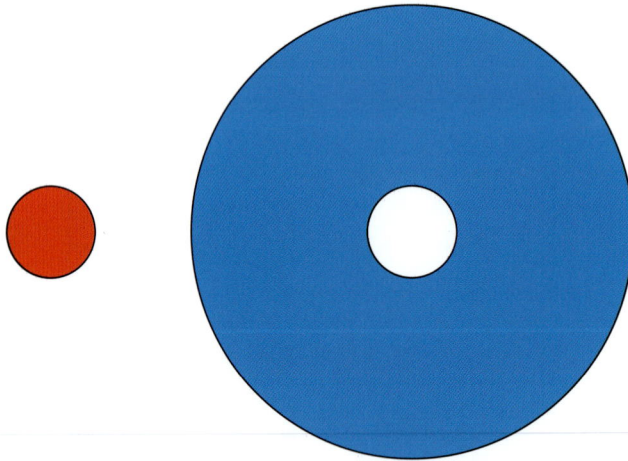

Do the same thing with these four glasses and two red
balls. (Or are there six glasses and three red balls?)

What happens?

Each eye sends a picture to your brain, which mixes the two pictures into one clear picture. Normally, both eyes look at the same thing, but when you look at something close up, your brain cannot always sort out the two pictures correctly.

You may see bits of both pictures on top of each other. Sometimes you see more than is really there, like the glasses and the balls. Sometimes you see less.

Mixing colours

1 Hold the book about 30 cm away.
2 Look at the white star. Bring the book closer.
3 You may see two stars and three triangles.
   The middle triangle may look green – a mixture of yellow and blue.

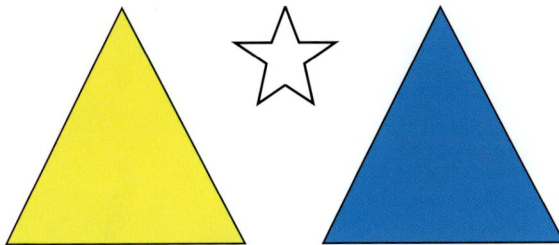

3D photographs

When you look at something, the two pictures seen by your eyes are not exactly the same, because your eyes are about 5 cm apart. Your brain uses the differences in the two pictures to tell you if something is close to you or distant.

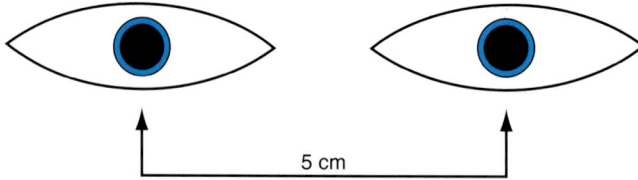

Ordinary photos are flat. They have just two **dimensions** (height and width). If you have two photos, taken about 5 cm apart, you can arrange them so that your brain sees them in the way your eyes would normally see things. Your brain uses the differences in the photos to add the third dimension (3D) – depth.

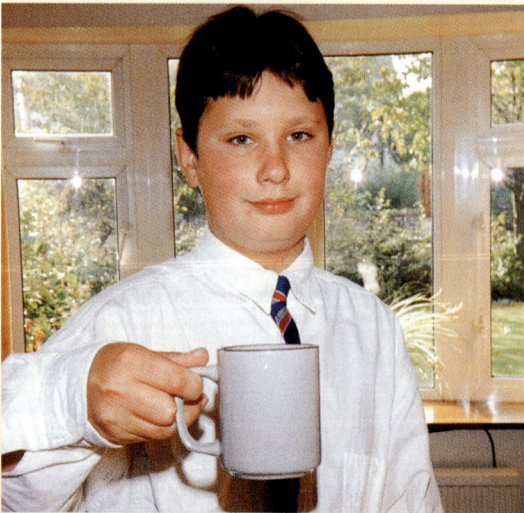

Picture seen by one eye

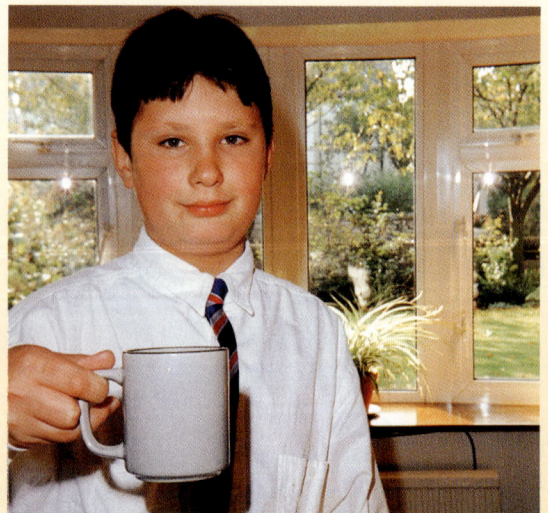

Picture seen by the other eye

How to look at the 3D photos on pages 28 and 29

You will need

- a mirror, at least 15 cm high and at least 10 cm long
- 3D photos on pages 28 and 29

1 Hold the mirror with its **reflecting** side on the right. Put the mirror's short edge between the two pictures.

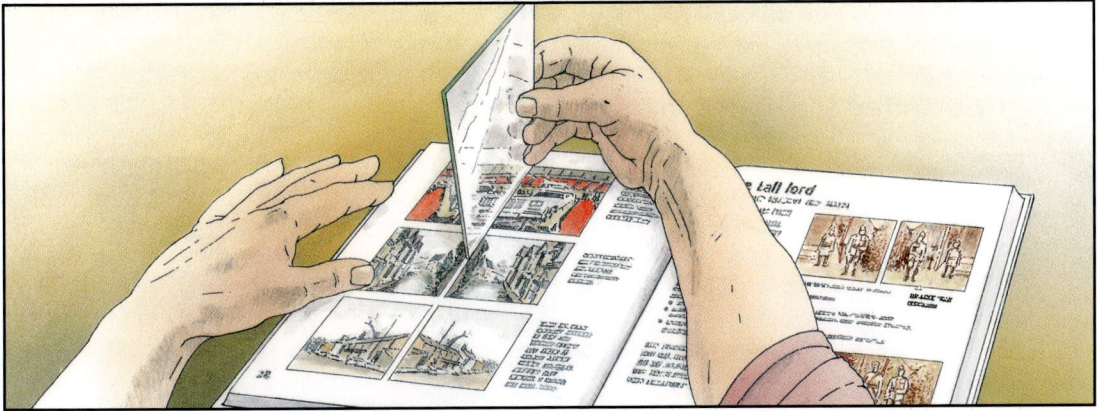

2 Put your nose over the top edge of the mirror. Look at the photo on the left. (Your left eye looks at the photo on the left. Your right eye looks into the mirror at the reflection of the photo on the right.)

3 After a short time, you should see just one photo in 3D!

This is the longest car in the world. The picture was taken at the Motor Show in Birmingham.

This is an old house on the river, in Canterbury, Kent.

This is not an optical illusion! A man in Oxford really did build a giant model shark into his roof! The shark is made of fibreglass.

The tall lord

This is another 3D photo. You can look at it with a mirror, like the ones on page 28.

This photo was taken in 1900. It shows Lord Roberts with his Indian servant.

In the photo, Lord Roberts looks taller than the servant, but this is an **illusion**. Lord Roberts was short. The photographer created this illusion by:

- asking Lord Roberts to stand near the camera
- placing the camera low down, so that it looked up at Lord Roberts
- asking the servant to stand about 2 m behind Lord Roberts.

This is how Lord Roberts and his servant would have looked with the camera at normal height, and the two men side-by-side.

The horrible twitching finger!

Create your own **optical illusion**. You can make people think they can see a finger twitching in a box. What they really see is the end of your finger in a box.

1 Cut a hole in the bottom of the box, near one end. Make the hole big enough for your finger.

2 Put your finger through the hole.

3 Put the cotton wool around your finger, so people cannot see the hole.

4 For an extra-horrible effect, use paint or tomato sauce for "blood stains".

5 Put the lid on the box. Ask people if they want to see the horrible thing in your box. Take the lid off. Twitch the finger and watch them jump back in horror!

Tell your friends that they should never believe their eyes.

Glossary

camouflage the colouring or shape of a creature which helps it blend into its surroundings

dimension length (or width), height and depth are the three dimensions of an object

hexagon shape with six straight sides

illusion something seen which is not really as it appears

optical to do with sight and the eyes

rectangular with four straight sides and four right angles

reflecting showing an image; the shiny side of a mirror

transparent lets light and colour pass through it

wedge-shaped shaped with one thick end and one thin end

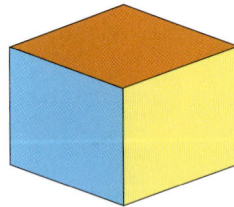

Index

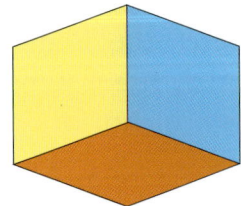